SAINT WENCESLAS
PRINCE OF BOHEMIA

Imprimatur.

Pragae, die 16. Januarii, 1929.

No. 777.

† ANTONIUS PODLAHA
Episcopus Paphiensis,
vicarius generalis.

THE LIFE
of
SAINT WENCESLAS

By
THE REV. FR. DVORNÍK, M.A., D.D.,
PROFESSOR OF THEOLOGY AT THE CAROLINE UNIVERSITY, PRAGUE.

Issued to Commemorate
THE MILLENARY of the SAINT'S MARTYRDOM

PRAGUE MXMXXIX

THE LIFE OF ST.WENCESLAS
THE LEGENDS

THE BEGINNINGS of the history of practically every modern nation are reflected in the legends woven round the national heroes and saints through whom the people were converted to the Christian faith, and to whom they frequently owe the foundations of their civilization generally.

The folk in their primal enthusiasm and gratitude surrounded such saints and heroes with the nimbus of legendary deeds, and gave them a place upon the altars of the churches which they had just begun to build. In the ages that succeeded, their memory became sanctified, for in them the nation saw the symbol of its own life. Their names became the watch-words of the armies in battle against the country's foes, and in times of peace they seemed the necessary mediators between God and the nation.

Even the modern historian and critic must approach these figures with respect. He may, of course, put to the test those beautiful legends with which the Middle Ages surrounded the lives of its saints. He has the right to track these legends to their very sources and reveal the characters as they actually were. It may be that his critical hand will somewhat dim the halo which an age of simplicity imparted to its saints, but he would certainly go beyond his duty were he to despise the sentiments of respect and confidence which the Middle Ages manifested, as legends show, in the saintly men of that period. It was often a devout confidence in the aid of its saints that profoundly influenced the nation's history and destinies.

Such is the spirit in which these few pages on the life of St. Wenceslas and on the early religious life of the Czechoslovak nation are written. While subjecting the matter of the individual legends to unsparing criticism, an endeavour has been made to preserve an atmosphere of admiration for the Saint, and to maintain that spirit of popular gratitude that breathes from all the legends that have come down to us.

These stories are fairly numerous. The first biography of St. Wenceslas was written shortly after his death in the Slavonic tongue and in the glagolic characters invented by St. Cyrill. Three recensions of this biography are extant. The first was issued in 1827 by the Russian Vostokoff, a second, somewhat abbreviated, is preserved in various Croat glagolic breviaries, while the third was published in 1883 by the Russian Archeological Commission. A shorter biography of St. Wenceslas, coupled with an account of the transfer of his remains, is to be found in the Old-Slav Collection of Lives of the Saints, the so-called *Prologue.* In the Greek Church this Collection is known as the *Synaxarion.*

The number of lives in Latin, emanating from the X. century is considerable, and some of them are of special importance. The oldest is one known from its opening words as the *Crescente fide.* It has come down to us in two versions, one Czech and the other Bavarian, which betray their origin by a number of divergencies on the question of race or nationality. This life was intended to show contemporaries that Bohemia was a civilized land, having already two saints, Ludmilla and Wenceslas. In the eyes of contemporaries this was the best proof that Bohemia was on a level with the countries of the European West, a thesis which received confirmation by the raising of Prague (about the year 973) to the dignity of a bishopric. St. Wenceslas enhanced the prestige of Bohemia within the framework of the German Empire. It is an interesting fact that another biography of St. Wenceslas was compiled about the same time by Gumpold, Bishop of Mantua, at the request of the Emperor Otto II. Gumpold limited himself for the most part to transcribing and amplifying the story as told in the *Crescente fide.*

St. Adalbert, Bishop of Prague from 982 to 997, also contributed to raising the prestige of Bohemia at the end of the X. century. Adalbert was a scion of the princely family of the Slavníks who were related to the ruling German dynasty. He acquired what learning was available in his day, and was an outstanding personality in every way. He was an admirer of the monastic ideal of Clugny, and being in close and unbroken contact with the then important centre of culture in the West — Monte Cassino — and with his friend the Emperor Otto III. was a leading figure in the so-called Othonian renaissance. To the brisk intercourse between Bohemia and Monte Cassino at this period we are indebted for the compilation of a new legend of St. Wenceslas in this venerable Italian monastery by the monk Lawrence.

Adalbert could not, of course, see St. Wenceslas honoured more abroad than at home. At his request the monk Christian, one of his relatives and a connection of the reigning house in Bohemia — if not a son of Boleslav himself, the Saint's brother — wrote an admirable life of St. Wenceslas, the best of all that have come down to us. The classical style of this life reveals an astonishing level of culture in Bohemia of that period, and provides several proofs of the existence of the Slavonic liturgy in Bohemia after the fall of the Great-Moravian empire. Christian corrects in more than one place the previous lives, the *Crescente fide* and the biographies by Gumpold and Lawrence. As his authorities he quotes contemporaries and notes made by St. Adalbert. Although this manuscript is one of the most important documents of Czech history, its lot has been not a little singular.

Christian's Life of St. Wenceslas was published first by *Balbin* in the year 1677, and after him by the Bollandists in their huge work, the *Acta Sanctorum. Dobrovský*, the famous Slavonic scholar, however, declared it to be a compilation dating from the XIV. century. Many other Czech historians accepted Dobrovský's opinion, but recently the eminent Czech historian, Dr. *Joseph Pekař* has illuminated the point in two works, one in Czech entitled *Nejstarší kronika česká* (Prague, 1903), and the other in German entitled. *Die Wenzels- und Ludmilalegenden und die Echtheit Christians* (Prague, 1906), proving that in Christian's work we possess a very valuable document dating from the X. century and written at the behest of St. Adalbert. In his two works, Dr. Pekař has examined the story of St. Wenceslas in the light of modern criticism.

It was probably also in Italy that there was composed as the beginning of the XI. century another life of the Saint, known as the *Oportet nos fratres*. It follows the work of Gumpold and in rhymed prose enumerates the virtues of its subject.

Gumpold's work was also, at the end of the X. or at the commencement of the XI. century, translated into Old Russian. The manuscript was recently found by Professor Nikolski in the Monastery of Borovsk.

The cult of the Saint which was popular in the XIII. century prompted the compilation of two other lives, the one commencing with the words *Oriente iam sole,* and the other with *Ut annuntietur.* Connected with the *Oriente iam sole* is the story of St. Wenceslas in the rhymed Chronicle of Dalimil. Finally, still another life was composed by the Emperor Charles IV. himself, the King of Bohemia, and was written in the XIV. century when Bohemia was at the height of its prosperity. It opens with the words *Crescente religione christiana.*

The works enumerated are the most important sources for the history of St. Wenceslas. A more detailed list may be found in the works of Dr. *Joseph Pekař,* in *F. Stejskal's* Life of Saint Wenceslas (Prague 1924), as well as in works which treat of the early period of Bohemian history generally, notably in *Novotný's* History of Bohemia (Prague, 1905). Since 1924, *Msgr.*

Podlaha, Coadjutor Bishop of Prague, has published in the Czech Clergy's Review *(Časopis kato-
lického duchovenstva)* a copious document-
ation of St. Wenceslas and his cult.

AT THE DAWN OF CZECHO-SLOVAK HISTORY.

THE DIM BEGINNINGS of the history of the Czech nation are illuminated by the names of its national heroes. St. Cyrill and St. Methodius, St. Wenceslas, St. Ludmilla, St. Procop, St. Adalbert, the blessed Mlada and Agnes mark the first stages of its evolution. These names, indeed, served to introduce the nation to the civilized world of that day. Their altars were on more than one occasion the refuge where the inhabitants of Bohemia sought sanctuary in the hour of danger. The memory of these glorious servants of God and of the nation was transmitted from father to son as a precious heritage, and it deserves to be held in honour by their descendants to-day, forming as it does an integral part of their national and religious patrimony.

14

In order properly to appreciate the life of St. Wenceslas it is essential to acquaint oneself with the activities of the Sts. Cyrill and Methodius, two names that evoke a brief but glorious past. These two brothers, Greeks of noble birth, issuing from the literary and religious renaissance of Byzantium in the first half of the IX. century, equipped with all the knowledge that men of learning in those days could acquire, and playing an important rôle in the life of their Church and their country, abandoned everything — the land of their birth, their monastery, their post as teachers, and the brilliant cultivated society of Byzantium — in order to go forth to carry the Gospel to the Moravians, distant tribes settled in the valley of the river Moravia and in the present Slovakia between the Danube and the Carpathians.

The ruler of the Moravians, Rastislav, had appealed to the Emperor Michael III. at Byzantium and to his uncle Barda to send him missionaries speaking the Slavonic tongue. With considerable political astuteness, Rastislav perceived the necessity of his people becoming Christian, but he did not desire this to entail the loss of their national and political liberties. Such danger actually existed, for the Germanic Empire, overflowing with the vitality of a young nation and embued with religious zeal, was seeking new spheres for its superfluous energies. Its path of conquest lay eastward. Having reduced the Saxons, the Empire was brought into direct contact with the Slavonic tribes settled along a frontier extending from the Baltic Sea, betwixt the Elbe and the Saal, touching the Bohemian Forest, the Danube, the Alps and following the Tagliamento to the Adriatic. All this unorganized area was bound, sooner or later, to succumb, for one of the characteristic faults of the Slavs, remarked on with astonishment by Byzantine writers themselves, was their lack of any sense of unity and political organization.

Only once since their settlement in these parts had the Slavs succeeded in forming a sort of empire, and the man who had united them

I.

(Samo, about the year 623) was not a Slav but a Frank. It was only the bitter lot to which they were subjected under their rulers at that period — the Avars — that roused the Slavs to the necessity of union. As long as Samo lived he was able to maintain his empire and even to beat off the attacks of his compatriots, the Franks, and in particular those of King Dagobert. His empire collapsed, however, immediately on the death of its founder. So little did this empire contribute to the subsequent development of the Slavs in these parts that even the extent of its frontiers is unknown to us. Historians can only assume that the Bohemia of to-day was part of it.

It is therefore all the more surprising that towards the middle of the IX. century the prince of one of these Slav tribes should have been able to group the Slavs of the Moravia valley into a sort of State. It was this formation which was to prove a serious obstacle to the hitherto victorious march of the German Empire eastwards. The resistance was soon to become a menace, for Rastislav compelled other Slav tribes to submit and join him. When the two Greek brothers arrived in Moravia in 863 they quickly grasped the situation. They endeavoured to give this new politital power a cultural foundation. They invented a special Slavonic script (known as the glagolic), they translated the lives of the Saints into Slavonic and introduced a Slavonic liturgy. Their work seemed full of promise, and even the Popes Hadrian II. and John VIII. supported the endeavours of Methodius, who continued to carry out the programme after the death of Cyrill at Rome. A vast diocese was created for him, embracing the whole territory of Great Moravia and Pannonia as far as to Serbia and Bulgaria.

The Germanic Empire regarded these developments with uneasiness. It succeeded in removing Rastislav through the treason of his nephew *Svatopluk,* but under the energetic hand of the new prince the menace to the Germans increased. In effect, a new Slavonic Empire uniting under one prince all the Slav tribes from the Bohemian Forest to the river Theiss had arisen. The Slavs slowly gained a consciousness of their own powers, and it is not difficult to understand the efforts made from now on by the Empire to rid itself of its dangerous rival. In this it succeeded after the death of Svatopluk, for despite the heroic resistance of his successor, *Mojmír II.*, Great Moravia succumbed about the year 906 to the simultaneous onslaughts of the Germans and of a new enemy in the Magyars. The young State disappeared for ever, leaving scarcely a trace behind it.

This political catastrophe had been preceded by a turn of affairs in the religious sphere. Even Rome had yielded to the insistence of the Germans, and Stephen V., a victim of the intrigues of the German clergy, reversed the policy of his predecessors Hadrian II. and John VIII. On the death of Saint Methodius (April 6th 885) he prohibited the use of the Slavonic liturgy.

The dream had been too splendid to last.

The Slavonic Empire was too young to resist the onslaughts of its more powerful rival. It had become a menace in the eyes of the Germans and had to disappear. The Germanic Empire had now free access to the East and proceeded to envelop the Slavs.

Such in brief are the memories invoked by the names of St. Cyrill and St. Methodius. The name of St. Wenceslas dominates the second phase of Czech history, after the ephemeral episode of Great Moravia. The two phases are so intimately connected that even Christian, who wrote the best life of St. Wenceslas (in the X. century) introduces his work with an exposition of the history of Moravia and an account of the two saints of Salonica.

Bohemia, like Moravia, stood in the way of German penetration to the East. She was in an even more dangerous situation than Moravia. The division into small tribes was still more pronounced, and the process of centralization under the aegis of a single ruler — of the Premyslide dynasty and Prince of the Czech tribe settled round Prague — made much slower progress. The Germans were at the very gates of the land, and having subjugated the Slavs of the North, Bohemia's neighbours, they represented a direct menace to the Slavs settled along the valleys of the Elbe and Vltava. In the reign of Svatopluk, Bohemia had been compelled to join the Moravian Empire. It was thence that she received the Christian faith. Her first Christian prince was *Bořivoj*, the grandfather of St. Wenceslas. He was baptized, as we learn from Christian and others, with his consort Ludmilla, by St. Methodius. Together with the Christian faith, Bohemia also received the foundations of Slavonic culture which had been brought to Moravia by St. Methodius and his brother.

The conversion of Bohemia to Christianity was not accomplished, however, without resistance — as is proved by the internal struggles which filled the years that followed. The pagan party — if we are to credit the picturesque recital of Christian — did not yield quietly. Their resistance was such that Bořivoj did not venture to construct the first Christian church in Prague where he resided, but chose Levý Hradec. The opposition of the pagan party was broken down with difficulty. Slavonic priests, trained by Methodius, preached the faith in rivalry with priests of the Latin school, emissaries of the Germanic Empire.

In the reign of Svatopluk the efforts at union among the Slav tribes in Bohemia made a certain measure of progress. Soon after his death, however, Bohemia detached herself from Great Moravia. *Spytihněv*, son and successor of Bořivoj and uncle of St. Wenceslas, had to acknowledge a kind of supremacy on the part of the Germanic Empire in place of the overlordship of Moravia (895), and the German influence became preponderating. It was supported and extended mainly by the Latin priests from the German lands. It is Spytihněv whom the German chroniclers cite as the first Christian prince in Bohemia, for they refused to acknowledge the work of St. Cyrill and St. Methodius.

The collapse of Great Moravia rendered this situation a permanent one, and established the ecclesiastical supremacy of Ratisbon. Nevertheless, thanks to the Slav clergy who passed over to Bohemia after the disappearance of Great Moravia, the Slavonic liturgy maintained its existence for many years. It was doomed, however, to disappear, for, having no bishop, the Slav clergy had no means of recruiting their ranks.*)

*) A detailed account of these events the reader will find in my book «Les Slaves, Byzance et Rome au IXe siècle», Paris 1926.

THE EARLY YEARS OF SAINT WENCESLAS.

WRATISLAV, THE BROTHer of Spytihněv, governed a part of the country — probably to the Northwest of Prague — subject, of course, to Spytihněv's overlordship. His consort was *Drahomíra*, of the family of the Stodorans, an important branch of the tribe of *Lutici*, later celebrated for their desperate resistence to Christianity and defence of national liberties. Drahomíra was a Christian, but she had retained something of the wild spirit of her race. Of her union with Wratislav there sprang, if we are to believe the legend, a family of seven children.

Wenceslas was the eldest son and had two brothers, Boleslav and Spytihněv. The latter seems to have died early, for there is only one mention of him. Of the four daughters, only the name of one, Přibyslava, has come down to us.

Wenceslas was born about the year 907, 908 possibly, as tradition says, at Stochov near Libušín. He was probably baptized by a Slavonic priest, one of the disciples of St. Methodius. One such priest — called Paul in the legends — lived at the court of Ludmilla, the grandmother of St. Wenceslas. It is he who was likewise the boy's first teacher, and it was from him that St. Wenceslas learnt his letters in Slavonic — doubtless at Tetín, a castle belonging to his grandmother. It was necessary, however, to provide the future prince with a wider education. At that period there existed in Bohemia a sort of college at the Castle of Budeč, near the Church of St. Peter, which had been built by Spytihněv. According to the legend, Uceno, a priest and probably of Czech origin, taught Latin there to the sons of the nobles. At this institution St. Wenceslas acquired Latin, the international language employed by the cultivated class of that day. The legends are unanimous in paying tribute to his intelligence and industry.

At the same time the young prince was instruct-
ed in the use of arms and other accomplish-
ments fitting a future ruler.

His father Vratislav succeeded Spytihněv on
that prince's death probably in 916. He had
previously assisted his brother in defending the
country against the incursions of the Magyars.
These Magyar incursions also menaced the Germanic Empire, and, coupled with the weak rule
of Louis the Child and Conrad I., resulted in
a loosening of the bonds which united Bohemia to the Empire. It was probably on one of
the expeditions against the Magyars that Vratislav met his death at the early age of 33 (about
920—921). His memory is perpetuated by the
Church of St. George which he built in close
proximity to the Castle of Prague.

Wenceslas was too young to assume the
responsibilities of government. He was at once,
however, acknowledged as prince, called to
reside at Prague, and installed by the people in
the throne of his father. «But because he was
still a minor», says Christian, «the nobles met

and wisely decided to place the prince and his brother Boleslav in charge of Ludmilla, of pious memory, the servant of Christ, for to educate them until by the grace of God they should arrive at full age and discretion». The reins of power were placed in the hands of Drahomíra, Vratislav's widow, until Wenceslas should be of age, that is, in all probability, until he was 18.

A new misfortune and a new grief were soon to afflict the young prince. A crime sullies the regency of his mother, who caused her mother-in-law Ludmilla to be assassinated. The motives for this dark deed, reflecting the semi—pagan morals of Czech society in the X. century, are obscure. The crime was a melancholy presage for Wenceslas.

The motives for the murder of Ludmilla were apparently various, and it would be unjust to lay all the responsibility upon Drahomíra. It would seem that she had been encouraged by a powerful party that had formed in Bohemia hostile to Ludmilla. The nobles, who had only superficially adopted Christianity, noted with disaffection Ludmilla's efforts to convert the country. They feared that the young prince, whose piety had already been remarked, would, under Ludmilla's influence, become «a monk rather than a ruler». It was not difficult for them to convince Drahomíra that Ludmilla was designing to get the reins of power into her own hands, that her influence upon Wenceslas was unfortunate, and that finally she favoured the formation of a party of priests and devotees whose activities would be disastrous for the country.

Drahomíra was no ordinary woman. She was energetic, ambitious and loved power. Her fiery character had been only imperfectly suppressed by the adoption of Christianity. Boundless ambition and jealousy drove her to crime. She was not content to see Ludmilla retire to Tetín Castle; she desired to get rid of her altogether. On the 16th of September 921 Ludmilla was strangled by two of Drahomíra's agents, Tunna and Gommon. Her grandson Wenceslas — so we read in his life — had foretold the martyrdom of his grandmother.

It is possible that material considerations had contributed to the crime, for Ludmilla's property was at once seized by the conspirators. None the less, religious motives lay in the main behind the deed. It will be remembered what difficulties were experienced by Bořivoj after his baptism. The pagan party was still very powerful. According to the earliest life of St. Wenceslas, the *Crescente fide*, and to Gumpold, pagan sacrifices were still frequently offered at this period, and the most powerful of the nobles took part in them. The young prince himself was invited to participate, but he always refused.

The attitude of the nobles towards the prince would seem to confirm our hypothesis. If the legends are to be credited, the party which had brought about the death of Ludmilla endeavoured to gain possession of the young prince too, for «he allowed himself to be corrupted by priests and was little better than a monk». The priests, whose zeal was common knowledge, were forbidden approach to him; they were even banished from the country and the young prince was prevented from indulging in religious exercises. He found it necessary to do his devotions in secret and to receive in the night the priests who encouraged him to remain true to the faith.

Christian relates that Wenceslas, on mounting the throne, bitterly reproached the nobles who had been his mother's counsellors, for their conduct towards him. «Wherefore, ye sons of evil-doers, ye liars and iniquitous persons», said he, «wherefore did ye hinder me from learning the divine law of our Lord Jesus Christ and obeying His commandments? If you find no pleasure in serving God, does this give you the right to prevent others? Till now I have been under your control. To-day I throw it off, and shall serve God with my whole heart.»

It will be seen that Wenceslas's youth was by no means devoid of incident. The young prince's character was formed amid suffering and self-sacrifice. Moreover, the death of Ludmilla did not mark the end of the end of the internal struggles that troubled the land. Drahomíra in the end found it necessary to deal severely with her former allies, Tunna and Gommon who, having acquired great power and influence after the murder of Ludmilla, became too independent for her. Suspecting Drahomíra's intentions Tunna succeeded in fleeing from the country, but Gommon was seized and perished with all his family. Here again, Drahomíra's cruelty reveals the morals of the semi-pagan society of the epoch.

The murder of Ludmilla made a deep impression on the people. They visited her tomb, and there was soon talk of the miracles which happened there. Drahomíra at once saw that these rumours could become a source of danger for her, and feared that public opinion would vent its displeasure upon her. Over Ludmilla's tomb she caused the Church of St. Michael to be built in order that — as the chroniclers say — the miracles might be attributed to the archangel.

These internal disorders did not improve

the young State's prestige. Arnulf, Duke of Bavaria, desiring to take advantage of them, invaded the country. What his object was, or what the result of the incursion was, we are not told. We only know that the invasion took place in the year 922. Perhaps the Duke desired to attach Bohemia to Bavaria and to the Empire. It is also possible that he wished to aid the head of the tribe of the Zličané, rival of the Czech princes, and to extend his dominion. Young Wenceslas undoubtedly took part in the defence of the country for, according to Gumpold, he addressed these words to the nobles: «With the help of God I have governed and defended the land, so far as in me lay, against its powerful foes.»

Whatever the result of this conflict was, the position of Bohemia was certainly shaken by it. It was a presage of the dire danger that was soon to threaten the country on the part of the Germanic Empire.

II.

THE SAINT'S REIGN.

UCH WAS THE SITUA-
tion in Bohemia in when
Wenceslas ascended the
throne. The country was
split by factions, and only
half Christianized, the am-
bitions of the chiefs of the
various tribes were increased by the interreg-
num under Drahomíra, and the prestige of
the prince was diminished. The danger threat-
ening from the Empire had already been fore-
shadowed by Arnulf's invasion. The danger
became still more menacing when *Henry the
Fowler* had established his authority. Bohemia
needed a firm hand and intelligent brain. A
great task awaited Wenceslas.

The young prince was 18 years of age when
he took over the reins of power about 925.
He had inherited the energy of his mother,
and his piety compensated for his lack of ex-
perience. The speech which — according to his

biographers, and especially Gompold — he addressed to his nobles on the day of his accession, fictitious though it may be, expresses well the sentiments which animated Wenceslas. He announces his firm determination to break completely with the party that had been the dominant factor during the regency of his mother. He declares himself thoroughly acquainted with the intrigues going on and that he will tolerate them no longer. «May the love of peace at home and abroad animate the country. Let the judges beware of hindering useful enterprises. Let no one again be guilty of the abominable crime of murder, so often committed by you. If the fear of the Supreme King does not keep you, O princes, from transgressing his law, know that our wrath will blaze up against such evildoers, and our zeal for the glory of God will visit with capital punishment all guilty of such crime.»

Wenceslas set about realizing his programme with a fervour and energy that merit our admiration. His biographers tell us that the rivalry between the two factions in the country still continued bitter. To put an end to it Wenceslas adopted a line of conduct that well reveals his character. When his friends accused Drahomíra of fomenting the troubles and even suggested that she was aiming at the life of Wenceslas and his brother, the prince compelled her to quit the Court, and to retire either to Budeč or abroad until order had been established in the land. One can easily imagine the effect that this gesture had upon the authors of the troubles. They had never anticipated such energy on the part of a young man whose whole life had apparently been passed in prayer and good deeds. Later, when calm was restored and Wenceslas was convinced that the accusations brought against his mother were false, he recalled her: «respectful of the divine command», says Christian, «which tells us to honour our father and our mother». She was never restored, however, to her former power. It would seem that, seeing the zeal of her son, Drahomíra reconciled herself with him, for the first legend declares: «she rejoiced in the faith of her son, and in the clemency he had shown.»

At the outset of his reign Wenceslas showed his filial piety in causing the relics of St. Ludmilla to be transferred from Tetín to Prague. Christian tells us that the body of the Saint had remained intact — a circumstance that greatly augmented the veneration with which she was regarded.

The change in the political regime was complete. The priests who had previously been driven from the country or at least deprived of their benefices were recalled. «The Church rejoiced», says Gumpold, «to live under such a prince, for she was not only restored by him but was also overwhelmed with his benefactions». The Latin legends of the X. century are unanimous in declaring that the news of the change of regime in Bohemia extended beyond the frontiers, so that «priests came in great numbers from Bavaria and from Svabia with relics of the Saints and very

III.

numerous books. Wenceslas bestowed upon them gifts of gold and silver, beautiful ornaments, and even clothes and other such things as they had need of. Wenceslas's teachers admired his sagacity, and declared he could say with the psalmist: «I have more understanding than all my teachers, for thy testimonies are my meditation».

All his biographers are likewise unanimous in lauding the saintly character of Wenceslas. Take, for example, what Christian, following the *Crescente fide* and the witness of Gumpold, says: «During Lent, and even in winter it was his custom to go barefoot over the steep and icy paths from castle to castle order to visit the churches of Christ, and people saw the blood-stained footprints that he left behind him. In order to preserve the chastity which he had vowed he wore a hair-cloth which has been preserved to our days in honour of him. Beneath the magnificent robes of royalty he wore a wollen garment like a simple monk, thus shining equally before God and man. He took but little food, passed much of the night in vigils and continuously rendered thanks to God. When it happened sometimes that he found himself in the midst of his nobles, like a lamb among the lions, and that he had drunk more than his wont in the late hours of the evening, he would rise early next morning and hasten to the nearest church. To the first priest or cleric whom he there encountered he would give his best robe and, casting himself at the priest's feet, would implore him instantly to pray to God for him, that God of his great mercy would forgive the sin of which he had been guilty the night before. He was assiduous at divine service, and daily made an offering which he had prepared with his own hands. At harvest time, accompanied by his faithful servant, he would go into the fields, cut some wheat and carry it home himself. He had a little hand-mill with which he ground the wheat, and taking some water — in the name of the Father, the Son and the Holy Spirit — mixed it with the corn and himself prepared

44

the host. He would go also to the vineyards, cull the grapes, press them with his own hands, and poured it into the pitcher, reserving the wine for the holy sacrifice.»

The accounts of the saintly character of St. Wenceslas grew, of course, with the lapse of time, and took on a legendary character. The pious biographer who wrote the *Ut annuncietur* at the close of the XIII. or the beginning of the XIV. century relates that during the winter it was the wont of the Saint to carry secretly to widows and orphans the wood that he cut in the forests unknown to the forester. The latter perceived that some one was stealing wood during the night, but was unable to discover the thief. He reported the matter to the prince. Wenceslas advised him to redouble his vigilance and to give the thief a good thrashing if he caught him, but to allow him to take the wood. The forester was surprised that the Saint should permit him to thrash anyone — a course very contrary to his habitual mildness. The next night the forester surprised the thief, but did not recognize him. He beat him so soundly that the Saint was hardly able afterwards to drag his load of wood with him. This happened on several occasions — so the biographer assures us. According to the same author, Wenceslas's servant, Podiven, who accompanied his master on these pious excursions, did not feel the cold when, during several frosts, he followed in the Saint's footprints. It was this legend that inspired John Mason Meale, the composer of the well-known Christmas Carol «Good King Wenceslas», which is very popular in England and in America.

Wenceslas devoted particular attention to a reform of the judicial system, taking part personally in the work of the courts. He endeavoured to bring about a reduction in the number of death sentences. When in his presence the judges were about to sentence a criminal to death, Wenceslas would leave the court under some pretext or other and hide himself, remembering the words of the Gospel: «Judge not, lest ye be judged». To limit the cases of capital punishment he had the gibbets destroyed and certain prisons closed — probably in places where the judges had not been regularly appointed by himself. At an epoch when morals were somewhat primitive and judges apt to pass sentence arbitrarily, the influence of the Saint's intervention must have been considerable.

The biographers further praise his kindly attitude in dealings with his subjects and his zeal to lead them to the path of truth. Christian adds a naive detail: «He would converse affably with the law-abiding but he showed a divine zeal in dealing with evildoers, vagabonds, drunkards and all who had departed from the path of virtue. When he could not reach them otherwise he would invite them at an opportune moment to his table and then beat them with thick rods, brandishing thus against the ancient enemy the buckler of Faith and the Lance of the Holy Spirit, which is the Word of God, in order to reduce to impotence the evil powers of this world. He was a true adorer of Christ, and, faithful to the precepts of the apostles, he reprimanded and exhorted unceasingly. He invited his subjects to attend the Supper of the Lord, and presented to Holy Mother Church the children whom he had rescued from the claws of Satan». In another place Christian records that St. Wenceslas would purchase pagan slaves in order to have them baptized — a fact which recalls the statement of the Arabian writer Ibraham ibn Jakub to the effect that in the X. century the city of Prague was an important centre of the slave trade.

Full of zeal for the conversion of his country, Wenceslas did not forget the building of churches to this end. Unfortunately the biographers only make mention of one founded by him, the Church of St. Vitus in close proximity to the Castle of Prague. He had it built with the concurrence of the Archbishop of Ratisbon whose diocese extended into Bohemia. The first Slavonic account of St. Wenceslas speaks in a general way of his having founded Christian churches.

We may assume with the majority of the accounts that St. Wenceslas preserved his chastity to the end of his life. The Old Slavonic legend that speaks of him having married is in this respect somewhat fantastic and confused and can hardly be accepted. There is found perhaps in Christian a passage which would seem to confirm what the Old Slavonic legend says, but historians are not unanimous in their interpretation of this passage. In any case it is in direct contradiction to another passage in Christian's account where it is categorically stated that Wenceslas kept his chastity to the end. Moreover, all the biographers attribute to the Saint the intention of going to Rome to enter a monastery, a step which would have been difficult had he possessed a wife.

This in rough outline indicates the religious activities of the Saint. It is unncessary to say that those activities contributed much to raise the moral level of the country and to assist in its civilization. Saint Wenceslas, however, was not only a Christian — he was at the same time also a prince and the military chief of his country. In this sphere, too, his activities, were productive of happy results.

IV.

THE POLITICAL ACTIVITIES OF ST. WENCESLAS.

THE BIOGRAPHERS HAVE of course very little to say about the Saint's political activities, for this point had practically no significance for them. Their object was to exalt his piety. From the little that we learn from them, however, it is clear that Wenceslas was by no means negligent of his responsibilities in respect of secular matters. The prince who had desired not to be present at the condemnation of a criminal, and who longed only for peace, was constrained to occupy himself in particular measure with his army. «He furnished his troops» — so his biographers tell us — «not only with the best possible arms but also with a suitable uniform.» Bohemia at that time had need of a well-disciplined army, for Wenceslas was obliged to draw his sword in the defence of his country. He was proably at the head of the troops when Arnulf invaded Bohemia during the regency of Drahomíra. At the same time, or possibly a little later, at the commencement of his own reign, he was called upon to protect his patrimony against the powerful tribe of the Zličané, who sought to profit by the troubles of Drahomíra's regency and to enlarge their territories at the expense of the tribe of the Czechs. Christian is the only one of the biographers who treats of this conflict in detail.

«The prince of the Castle of Kouřím, having gathered many people about him, began an insurrection against the Saint. Much blood flowed on both sides. Finally, it was proposed that the two leaders should decide the matter by single combat. When the two princes stepped forth for the fight, God caused the Duke of Kouřím to see a vision — the Holy Gross resplendent on the breast of Wenceslas. This miracle decided him, and he threw down his arms. Then he knelt at the feet of Wenceslas, and declared that none could vanquish one whom God miraculously protected. As he spoke the Saint raised him up and gave him the kiss of peace. Without further conflict Wenceslas confirmed his power over the prince of Kouřím and his castle, but permitted him to retain possession of it for the remainder of his life». We have here the story of one of Wenceslas's successful campaigns. A later chronicler, Dalimil, tells us that it was undertaken against a certain *Radislav*.

Wenceslas displayed great perspicacity in his dealings with the Germanic Empire. Henry the Fowler who had become king in 919, established his authority and signed a truce for nine years with Hungary whose invasions had of late seriously menaced the military power of the Empire. The old supremacy of the Empire was restored. Henry was finally in a position to put the strength of his armies to the test, and to resume the traditional policy of penetration eastwards, towards the lands inhabited by the Slavs. He proceeded on a concerted plan of campaign. Several tribes — the Bodrci, the Lutici and the Ratari — were early subjugated. In 928 it was the turn of the Stodoranes. In 929 Bohemia had to face the onslaught of the German armies. Henry and Arnulf easily overcame the troops guarding the frontier defiles and speedily appeared before Prague. What course was Wenceslas to take at this critical moment? His sagacious decision saved Bohemia. He saw that if hostilities continued the country would be devastated and suffer the same fate as the territories of those Slavs that had already been subjugated. He spontaneously resolved to submit and recognize the sovereignty of the Empire. He undertook to pay an annual tribute which later amounted to 500 pieces of silver and 120 oxen. Thus Bohemia was saved, for she would not long have been able to resist the German attacks. If they had forced the Germans to put them down by force of arms, the Czechs would have paid dear for an audacious resistance. Wenceslas realized this and preferred to com-

V.

promise. All historians recognize that in doing so he gave proofs of uncommon sagacity. He had a horror of war. Moreover he was on terms of close friendship with the Archbishop of Ratisbon, and there were, again, many German priests in Bohemia to whom, as already stated, Wenceslas's benefactions were numerous. All this explains why the Empire was satisfied with a pacific submission.

From now on Wenceslas continued on good terms with Henry I. The Emperor even made him a present of an arm of St. Vitus — this probably on the signing of the treaty of peace. It was this gift that decided the Saint to dedicate the church he had just commenced to build to St. Vitus and not to St. Emeram as was, according to the first Slavonic legend, his original intention.

Subsequent ages wove a fabric of romance round the relations of Henry and Saint Wenceslas. The *Oriente jam sole* of the XIII. century relates that on one occasion Wenceslas was to take part in the annual assembly of the princes of the Empire. All had arrived with the exception of Wenceslas who was delayed in church. Henry regarded his lateness as an affront, and forbade the other princes, on pain of death, to rise and give place to Wenceslas when he should appear. When Wenceslas entered the princes were amazed to see the Emperor himself rise, walk humbly towards the Saint, and lead him to a seat next the throne. In explanation of his strange conduct the Emperor related to the princes how he had beheld an angel accompanying the Saint, upon whose forehead shone a heavenly cross.

Another account, dating from the XIV. century, even affirms that Henry nominated Wenceslas King of Bohemia, but it is unnecessaty to have recourse to legendary accounts to form a high opinion of Wenceslas.

His deeds speak for themselves.

THE MARTYR'S DEATH.

ENCESLAS WAS UN-
able to conciliate all the dis-
affected among his subjects.
The time was too short for
the successful results of his
innovations to manifest themselves in full. The party who
had dominated during the regency of Drahomíra bore their overthrow with ill grace, and
waited for a suitable opportunity to take their
revenge. The zeal with which the young prince
sought to convert the whole country to Christianity irritated the nobles whose own conversion was often superficial and who had
little taste for spending their time in church.
In his fervour, Wenceslas forbade certain pagan usages which were deeply rooted in the
habits of the people, and in this way he roused
up new enemies. Possibly, too, the favours
which he showered upon the priests excited
the jealousy of the nobles. The latter, more-

over, did not approve of his policy of conciliation towards the Empire. They would have liked to offer armed resistance, and they accused the prince of weakness and cowardice. New dangers began to make Wenceslas's position critical, but it is possible that he would have triumphed over all, had not his enemies found a leader in the person of his own brother, Boleslav.

Boleslav had not had the advantage, as had Wenceslas, of the beneficent influence of Ludmilla. He was a true son of Drahomíra, who indeed had kept him away from Ludmilla, lest he should follow the example of Wenceslas. He was of a bold and enterprising spirit, rough and indomitable, and the characteristics which he had inherited from his mother were tempered by no piety. His passions were unrestrained and he disliked his brother — all the more so when the latter, as the legends tell us, attempted to bring him to a better mode of life. Cosmas, a canon, who wrote the first Czech chronicle (in the XI. century) relates a

62

significant fact, which, even if not true in all its details, is significant enough. Boleslav wished to construct a castle of stone at the confluence of the rivers Jizera and Elbe, and announced this to a gathering of the elders of his people. His people protested, as it was the custom at that period to build such castles only of timber. Rising in a rage, Boleslav seized his sword and cut off at one blow the head of the elder who had voiced the protest.

It is not to be wondered at that the malcontents throughout the country found their leader in Boleslav. Putting aside all hesitation he resolved to seize the power and get rid of Wenceslas by violence. He was able to count on numerous friends, and it is not improbable that he had the support of the pagan party. The motives for the murder of Wenceslas were thus several, and apart from the ambition of Boleslav, they were political as well as religious, though the latter undoubtedly dominated.

The conspirators were well aware that it would be difficult for them to carry out their designs in Prague itself, where Wenceslas possessed so many friends and faithful troops. They decided to lure him, therefore, to Stará Boleslav, the residence of his brother, where a trap could be more easily laid for him. Let us hear the description of the manner of the Saint's death from the pen of the pious Christian:

«All this happened in the reign of Henry of Saxony with whom Wenceslas was on terms of sincere friendship . . . . Boleslav's residence was the castle bearing his own name. The arrows of the Demon had touched him from every side, and he was tormented by the lust to rule. At the Feast of Cosmas and Damian, two days before the Feast of the blessed Archangel Michael, Boleslav, under the pretext of dedicating the church of his castle to the two saints, treacherously invited his brother to a banquet, or, as the events proved, to his death. St. Wenceslas was fully aware of his brother's designs, but tried to remain calm and courageous. He took leave of all who were united to him in the bonds of kinship or friendship, embraced and kissed them, and set out on his journey armed only with the weapons of faith.

When he arrived, the banquet was all in readiness, and the conspirators, some of them in hiding, were likewise present. Wenceslas proceeded to the Church and attended Mass. Then, commending himself to God and the Saints Cosmas and Damian, he returned, cheerful of spirit, to the banqueting hall. When the conspirators with murder in their hearts grew heated with food and wine, they stealthily drew their swords from beneath their garments . . . . thrice they stood up, and thrice sat down again, for God did not permit them to accomplish their design on that day, desiring perchance to let the following day (on which as yet no festival fell) become a Saint's day. Seeing those about him excited, the Saint rose and quitted the feast. One of his friends approached him and said: 'Quick, I have a horse ready, mount it and get away as speedily as possible, for death menaces you here!' Wenceslas, however, took no heed of these words but returned to the banqueting hall. Taking up a cup he drank out of it, saying to all present: 'Let us drink the cup to the honour of the blessed Archangel Michael, praying him to usher our souls into the peace and joy of life everlasting! And when all those faithful to him had responded' Amen', he drained the cup, embraced his friends and then retired to his chamber to rest. There he prayed long until, overcome by fatigue, he fell asleep».

The conspirators then determined to kill Wenceslas the next morning on his way to church. In order that he should be unable to seek sanctuary, Boleslav had ordered the priests to lock the church doors. «On the morning of the next day, Wenceslas — sacrifice offered to Christ — rose early to go to church as was his wont. He desired to be alone in order that he might pray long, and thus there is no doubt, fell into the snare laid by his enemies. For the priest of this church, a man of iniquity, seeing the man of God approach, locked the doors according to the orders given him. At this moment Boleslav and his fellow conspirators emerged from their hiding-place. Wenceslas embraced his brother, and thanking him, said: 'Mayst thou ever prosper, brother, and have abundance of the good things of this world and the next. May Christ invite thee to His eternal feast as thou hast so generously entertained me and my friends.' Haughty of spirit and with hatred in his eyes Boleslav drew the sword that was concealed beneath his cloak, and replied: 'Yesterday I served thee as I could, to-day behold how brother serves brother!' So saying he struck a blow at the Saint's head, but as God protected him the blood scarce flowed. The miserable Boleslav was greatly terrified at this and struck a second blow. Wenceslas caught the sword with his bare hand and said: 'Thou dost ill to strike me!' When he saw, however, that Boleslav blindly persisted in his design, he threw the sword at his feet saying: 'Man, condemned by thine own judgement seest thou not that I could crush thee like an insect? But the right hand of servant of God may not be stained with the blood of a brother.' Raising the sword he returned it to his brother, and hastened towards the church. Boleslav, however, pursued him, crying: 'Friends, friends, where are you? You serve your lord ill, abandoning him in such peril.' A horde of evil men armed with swords and spears rushed out of their ambush and struck Wenceslas down at the door of the church. The saintly soul, freed from the trammels of this world, surrounded with the aureole of the martyr, betook itself to its Lord on the 28th of September in the year of Grace 929».

Such is Christian's account, and it is probably the one which most nearly approaches the truth. The death of the Saint was a signal for the persecution of all those who had been his friends. Even his mother Drahomíra did not feel safe. In all probability she had been present at the banquet given by Boleslav, and when she learnt of the horrible crime she hastened to the fatal spot, took the corpse of Wenceslas and, assisted by a few friends, hid it in the church. Fearing the wrath of Boleslav, she then fled beyond the frontiers of Bohemia, taking refuge in Croatia, there to expiate the crime of which she herself had been guilty — the murder of Ludmilla.

The fratricide had the body of the Saint interred in all haste by the priest Paul, the same, in all probability, who had buried Ludmilla, and hurried to Prague to seize the reins of power. Many of the partisans of Wenceslas were killed or imprisoned or compelled to quit the country. Among the last-named was the old servant and faithful friend of Wenceslas, *Podiven*. He returned later to Bohemia, and slew one of his master's murderers. He was seized by Boleslav, however, and hanged on the spot. Subsequently he was venerated as a martyr.

The priests who had previously enjoyed the favour of Wenceslas, had now much to suffer. The foreign priests were obliged to leave the country, and wherever they went they described Boleslav as cruel and a pagan. This explains how later historians were led to regard Boleslav as a pagan to the end.

THE CULT OF THE SAINT.

HE TRAGIC DEATH OF Wenceslas not only increased the veneration in which he was held, but it also brought about a change in the sentiments of those who had been discontented with his reign. Before long people began to talk of the miracles which took place at his tomb, and his fame spread not only throughout the whole country but even beyond its borders — thanks, above all, to the priests whom Boleslav had driven forth. It was perhaps this popular veneration for Wenceslas which led to a certain change of attitude on the part of Boleslav, and caused him to show more respect to the remains of his brother. The body was interred under the walls of the Church of SS. Cosmas and Damian at Stará Boleslav. This small church was soon enlarged, with the result that the tomb of Saint Wenceslas was now inside the church itself. The people, however, continued to demand that the relics of the Saint should be transferred to Prague. Boleslav ceded to the popular demand and on the 4th of March 932 the Saint's body was brought to the Church of St. Vitus, the construction of which had been commenced by Wenceslas himself. According to the biographers, the body had suffered no disintegration. The miracles which took place during the transference of the body from Boleslav to Prague still further increased the veneration in which the Saint was already held.

What has been said in the introduction concerning the most important legends shows how widespread was his cult and the sense of the services rendered to his nation after his death. His martyrdom supplied writers of that epoch with a popular subject, and contributed to the development of literary activities. Nor should the miracles attributed to him be lightly passed by. He was invoked as the consoler and liberator of captives and prisoners — this corresponding with the zeal he had shown in reforming the judicial system of the country. Among the cases of healing attributed to him, the *Crescente fide,* as well as the accounts by Gumpold and Christian, refer to a paralytic who came «from the Frankish land». This man was brought by merchants to Prague and there, thanks to the intercession of the Saint, recovered his faculties. The fame of his sanctity had thus early spread to distant parts.

Wenceslas was canonized at an early date, probably by the first Bishop of Prague, Dĕt-mar, or by St. Adalbert. As is well known, the act of canonization at this epoch was not yet reserved to the Pope. A sacramentary of the reign of Otto III. (993—1002) and of St. Wolfgang (994) already fixes the 28th of September as the Saint's day. In Bohemia, moreover, the Feast of St. Wenceslas has always been observed on that day.

Wenceslas was soon regarded as the national hero of the Czechs. Very shortly after his death his subjects were able to realize that the policy he had pursued towards the Empire was the only feasible course to take in the circumstances. At the outset of his reign, Boleslav, his brother, did not venture to adopt any other. It was only after the death of Henry I. (936) that he openly refused to pay the annual tribute. For 14 years he vainly strove to maintain a complete independence of the Empire, but in 950 he was compelled once more to recognize the sovereignty of the Empire and to revert to the policy inaugurated by his brother. This remained the traditional policy in Bohemia, which, though nominally forming a part of the Empire, enjoyed an exceptional position. Despite invasions from time to time, Bohemia was able to develop a national and economic life of her own, and her dukes and kings frequently possessed a preponderating influence in the Empire during the Middle Ages.

Wenceslas also became the patron and protector of the Czech armies. His lance, borne at the head of the troops, ensured victory. The chronicle compiled by Cosmas and his suc-

VI.

cessors gives many examples of the aid rendered by the Saint. In the year 1002, during the occupation of Bohemia by the Poles. «Christ remembered his Czechs», and with the aid of St. Wenceslas, their lawful duke, Oldřich, was able to regain his country. It was also the aid of St. Wenceslas, which enabled Břetislav I. to win an important victory over the Emperor Henry III. near Domažlice. Again in 1126, when King Lothar wished to interfere in the affairs of Bohemia and oppose the legitimate prince, Soběslav, his army, thanks to St. Wenceslas, was routed at Chlumec. In the reign of King Přemysl Otokar II., one of the greatest rulers of the Přemyslide dynasty, the army against the Hungarians was placed under the protection of the Saints Wenceslas, Adalbert and Procop. The battle which ensued at Kressenbrunn (1260) near the confluence of the rivers Moravia and Danube ended in the defeat of the Hungarians. The detachment which carried the standard of St. Wenceslas suffered no loss of any kind. It was again to St. Wenceslas that was due the victory gained by King Wenceslas II. at Sieradze in 1292. The warlike John of Luxembourg, the King of Bohemia who was later to lose his valiant life aiding the French against the English at the battle of Crecy, won on Saint Wenceslas's Day in 1322 a victory over Frederick the Handsome at Mühldorf.

Under John's son, Charles IV., Emperor of the Holy Roman Empire and friend of Pope Clement, Bohemia attained the height of her power and prosperity. This pious king was a particular admirer of Saint Wenceslas. He neglected no opportunity of embellishing the Wenceslas Chapel in the Cathedral of St. Vitus, which he was building to replace the ancient church built by the Saint. The crown of Bohemia which he had made, was to be placed on the skull of St. Wenceslas, and is thus known as the crown of St. Wenceslas. For the safe keeping of the crown jewels Charles IV. built the Castle of Karlův Týn (Karlstein), which still contains handsome frescoes illustrating the life of Saint Wenceslas. From the reign of Charles there date also the finest monuments, canvases and statues of the Saint, among them the well-known statue in the St. Wenceslas Chapel, the work of the sculptor Peter Parler.

At Rome, too, the cult of the Saint was not unknown at this period. The Bishop of Olomouc, Berka de Duba, had an altar erected to St. Wenceslas in the Basilica of St. Peter, and endowed it with a foundation. To-day there exists but one copy of the altar picture of the Saint — preserved in the Vatican.[1])

In all Czech churches there is still sung the «St. Wenceslas Anthem», one of the most important and interesting evidences of the cult of the Saint in the XIII. and XIV. centuries.

[1]) Another copy of this picture is the work of the Czech artist Hynais. It is now at Treviso (Umbria) in the Chapel of St. Wenceslas. The altar of the Saint in the Basilica at Rome was erected in the year 1630. Until 1743 it was adorned by a picture painted by the famous Angelo Carossella. This picture was then transferred to the Quirinal, and the altar received a mosaic copy by Christopher Romano. A further picture of the Saint is to be found in Rome — in the Church of Notre Dame Trastevere.

It retains its archaic form, as is to be seen from the first four stanzas, of which the following is a translation:

> Saint Wenceslas;
> Duke of Bohemian lands,
>   Our Prince,
>   Pray to God for us,
>   And to Holy Spirit.
>   Kyrie eleison.
>
> O, Thou Inheritor of Bohemia,
> Remember thy race, thy people,
>   Suffer not us
>   Nor our children to perish
>   Saint Wenceslas,
>   Kyrie eleison.
>
> We implore thy succour,
> Have pity upon us,
>   Console the sad,
>   Drive all ill away,
>   Saint Wenceslas,
>   Kyrie eleison.

Heaven's Court is beautiful,
Happy they who enter
   Into Life eternal,
   The shining light
   Of Holy Spirit.
   Kyrie eleison.

This chant was augmented by several further stanzas in the XIV. century, and became national. It was sung indeed in the camps of the Hussites, for even in that period of confusion and civil strife, the nation did not forget its Saint. The Hussites invoked St. Wenceslas, and attributed their successes to him. The legend of the knight visible from afar on his white steed and fighting at the head of the army appears again in the account of the Battle of Chlumec, where the German army was defeated by the Hussites. The Hussites also bore the image of St. Wenceslas as well as the words of the Wenceslas Anthem on their shields. It was again this anthem that the Czechs sang when they accepted in 1436 the «Compacts» which were to reconcile them once more with the Catholic Church. Finally, it was to the sound of this anthem that *George of Podiebrad* was proclaimed king in 1458.

During the nation's darkest period in the XVII. and XVIII. centuries, the cult of St. Wenceslas inspired the nation with courage. At the beginning of the XVII. century a large proportion of the population had become Protestant. The Battle of the White Mountain in 1618 saw the defeat of the Protestant nobility and the triumph of the House of Habsburg. The Saint's name was invoked to lead the people back to Catholicism. The Jesuits were indefatigable in founding schools and colleges, and numerous dramas were there played in which St. Wenceslas was the hero and was designed to present to the rising generation the ideal of a good Catholic. These plays likewise contributed largely to revive national sentiment.

A seminary for priests was also founded and placed under the patronage of St. Wenceslas.

At the close of the XVII. century there was established a «Society of St. Wenceslas» with the object of publishing religious books. This Society performed a great work, for Czech books were rare in the reigns of Marie Theresia and Joseph II.

When the era of national revival opened in the XIX. century it was once more in the cult of St. Wenceslas that the nation's sentiments found their best expression. The Czech delegates who proceeded to the Vienna Parliament in 1848 to uphold the nation's rights attended, previous to their departure from Prague, a mass celebrated before the statue of the Saint on the public square which is now called after him. His picture adorned the standards of many of the national guards constituted in that year. Strangers arriving at Prague never fail to admire the imposing equestrian statue of the Saint. It is the work of the celebrated Czech sculptor, Myslbek, and was unveiled in 1906. On the pedestal are inscribed the words of the prayer, frequently uttered by the nation in its dark hours: «Saint Wenceslas, suffer not us nor our children to perish!»

During the World War, when the nation's fate hung in the balance, the anthem of the patron Saint was frequently heard in the churches. Its singing was indeed prohibited by the Austrian Government who saw in it the expression of a national protest. The Czechoslovak legions that fought side by side with the Allies also placed themselves under the protection of the Saint. The first Czech battalion in Russia — the Česká družina — formed in 1914, had the picture of the Saint on its standard. The first Czech regiment formed in Russia in 1926 bore at first also the name of Saint Wenceslas.

The profound impression exercised by the cult of the Saint upon the nation was again evidenced after the war when the country had recovered its independence. By an Act of Parliament of the year 1923 the first gold coins to be minted were to bear the figure of Saint Wenceslas. It is assumed that it was he who minted the first Czech coins in existence, the so-called denars.

Throughout the thousand-years' existence of the Czechoslovak nation St. Wenceslas has thus been the symbol of its strength and the protector and patron of its people. He introduced his nation to the civilized world. The name of St. Wenceslas recalls even to the children of to-day the faith and religion of their fore-fathers. Never throughout the most troubled periods of the nation's history has St. Wenceslas been forgotten — the Father of his Country and Saint of the Catholic Church. It is round his black-eagled standard that the Czechs as ardent patriots have rallied through the ages, and the services he has rendered his nation are beyond computation.

Hence the desire of the whole nation to commemorate in worthy fashion the thousandth anniversary of his death. The climax of the celebrations will be the consecration of the Cathedral of St. Vitus. Built to replace the modest church erected by Saint Wenceslas, it

was commenced by the Emperor Charles IV,
King of Bohemia, when Bohemia was at the
height of its power and prosperity, and it
has now been completed. A happy symbol!
May the millenary of Saint Wenceslas prove
the point of departure for a religious revival
throughout the country as a worthy consum-
mation of the national and political renaissance.
«Saint Wenceslas, suffer not us nor
our children to perish!»

LIST OF ILLUSTRATIONS:

CONTENTS:

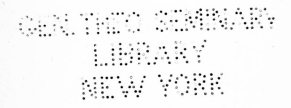

THIS LIFE OF ST. WENCESLAS IS PUBLISHED
BY THE COMMITTEE FOR THE COMMEM-
ORATION OF THE MILLENARY OF THE
SAINT. IT HAS BEEN PRINTED BY THE STATE
PRINTING OFFICE, PRAGUE, UNDER THE
CARE OF KAREL DYRYNK, WITH ORNA-
MENTATION BY ZDENKA BRAUNEROVÁ.
AN EDITION OF 400 NUMBERED COPIES,
PRINTED ON DUTCH VAN GELDER
PAPER, HAS ALSO BEEN ISSUED.

PRAGUE   A. D.   M C M X X I X